D1626985

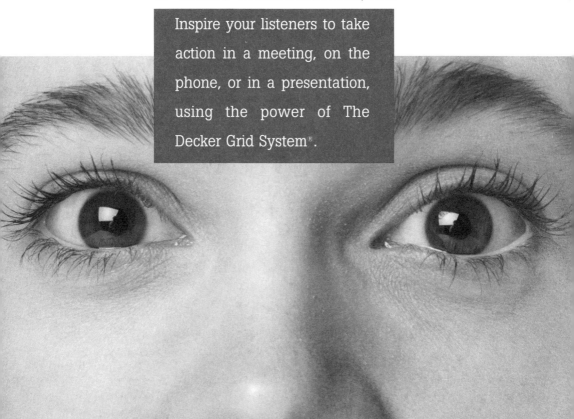

C R E A T I N G

messages

THAT

motivate

BY DECKER COMMUNICATIONS, INC.

Inspire your listeners to take action in a meeting, on the phone, or in a presentation, using the power of The Decker Grid System®.

CREATING MESSAGES THAT MOTIVATE

In this climate of high-velocity change, you often can't get the results you want alone. Daily, you need to be able to inspire those around you to do what's necessary to make the impossible a reality. Your personal and professional success is largely determined by what you say and how you say it.

Inspire your listeners to take action on the phone, in a meeting, or in a presentation, using the power of The Decker Grid System®

Spoken communication is the most effective way to move from ideas to action, and from action to results. It offers a potential that few of us use to our full advantage.

This Success Guide will help you improve what you say. It will teach you a system that ensures the messages you convey to others get results. It will change the way you communicate. It will make you a more powerful person.

We call our secret weapon The Decker Grid System® – a quick, efficient way to create messages that motivate. It was originally developed more than thirteen years ago to help participants in our communication skill building programs prepare their spoken messages more quickly and effectively. Since then, over 100,000 people have been positively affected by The Decker Grid System®.

The Decker Grid System® is quite a rigid-sounding name for what is, in fact, a very flexible and creative process. It is a guaranteed method for developing action-oriented messages that focus on the listener. What begins as a conscious tool becomes a way of thinking. This system uses several ideas you may be familar with and puts them together in a new way. Once you learn and then use this system for creating messages, you will:

- Dramatically reduce the time you take to decide what to say
- Avoid dumping data on unreceptive listeners
- Increase listener attention and retention of your information
- Speak confidently at a moment's notice
- Substantially improve your ability to move people to take your desired action

Whether it's a voicemail message, a presentation to a prospective client, your turn at the next staff meeting, or a one-on-one over coffee, you will dramatically increase your ability to engage the people around you to help you achieve your desired results.

This Success Guide is designed to give you the essentials for creating messages that motivate. It is written so that each section builds upon the previous one. Please read it through the first time from start to finish. After that, keep it as a handy reference and go directly to the section that covers the step where you need help. Call us if you have questions or comments. Our toll-free number is 1.800.547.0050. Our web site address is: http://www.decker.com.

I think of this system as "software for the mind"...still, by far, the mightiest computer.

Bert Decker

Bert Decker
San Francisco, California
June, 1996

C O N T E N T S

1 | What's Usually Missing

9 | First Some Basics...

18 | Lay the Cornerstones for Success

20 | ABC's of POV

22 | Audience: Walk A Mile In Their Shoes

25 | Actions: Show Them The Way

28 | Benefits: What's In It For Them?

31 | Now It's Time To CREATE

34 | CLUSTER Like Crazy

37 | COMPOSE Your Masterpiece

51 | Attention Getters & Memory Hooks

68 | Enough Preparation – Now Speak!

72 | Application One – Time For A Quickie!

73 | Application Two – Increasing Your Phone Power

74 | Application Three – Maximizing Your Meeting Effectiveness

76 | Application Four – Creating Presentations That Produce Results

78 | Application Five – Hosting A Successful All-Day Meeting

79 | Interacting With Your Visuals

80 | Use It Or Lose It!

82 | Tools To Make You A More Effective Communicator

WHAT'S USUALLY MISSING

When we speak with others, we often fail to include one or more of the key ingredients for success. Knowing what these ingredients are will help you understand the power of The Decker Grid System®, as it simply and systematically ensures these ingredients are present in every message you communicate.

MISSING INGREDIENT ONE

The power of the emotional connection. When you speak, you have the opportunity to communicate your emotion along with your information. It is your emotional connection that will move your message into the hearts and minds of your listeners. It is what brings life to the concepts you communicate.

Somewhere along the line, we learned that it's not okay to convey emotion in business. Perhaps what happens is that we take emotion to mean "emotional" and conjure up images of people weeping. Nonsense! Emotion is the energy that enables people to achieve greatness. Communicate your conviction! Develop a clear Point of View (POV).

PEOPLE BUY ON EMOTION
AND JUSTIFY WITH FACT

MISSING INGREDIENT TWO

What it means to the other guy. When you speak, your listeners listen through their own filters. Your key to success is to make certain that the message you deliver is so relevant to your listeners that you successfully capture and maintain their interest. Yet, it is easy to miss this key ingredient by becoming internally focused as you prepare to communicate about something that is important to you.

Later, we'll show you some easy ways to gain the listeners' perspective. Understanding your listeners is absolutely essential to the success of your message.

MISSING INGREDIENT THREE

We forget to be net. Like you, your listeners are on information overload. They often wonder how they're going to be able to manage the sheer mass of data that surrounds them. Give them the gift of brevity. Help them out. Net it out. They will thank you by listening to you, rather than the person who leaves five-minute voicemails. Keeping it simple and keeping it brief are just two of the wonders of The Decker Grid System®.

NO MAN PLEASES BY SILENCE; MANY PLEASE BY SPEAKING BRIEFLY.   - AUSONIUS

MISSING INGREDIENT FOUR

We don't tell them what to do. If the purpose of speaking is to influence others, then to be successful, we must indicate what actions we want our listeners to take. Sound obvious? Think back to the number of times you have been the listener and have found yourself saying, "Yes, now what?" Don't leave it to your listeners to interpret your intentions. S-p-e-l-l it out for them.

Vision without action is merely a dream. Action without vision just passes the time. Vision with action can change the world. – Joel Arthur Baker

MISSING INGREDIENT FIVE

The All-Important WIIFM. WIIFM – that is, "what's in it for **me**..." The number one way to motivate listeners to take action is to tell them how they will benefit. If you can't think of any benefits, think harder. There needs to be some sort of personal gain for your listeners in order to strike a responsive cord.

MISSING INGREDIENT SIX

Failing to make it two-way. When communication between people is only one-way, it is not as effective as an interactive exchange. The best way to build commitment in your listeners is to engage them in the process. Build in opportunities for dialogue. Ask questions, genuinely listen, and acknowledge their answers.

The Decker Grid System® provides the flexibility for two-way communication throughout the delivery of your message.

Knowing the importance of these missing ingredients sets the stage for introducing The Decker Grid System®. Before we launch into the Four-Step Process, let's first cover some basics...

FIRST SOME BASICS...

Choose the right medium for your message.
If the spoken and written word had the same effect, you could get everything you wanted in life from writing a good memo. They are different.

While writing can be detailed, logical, and organized, speaking effectively requires spontaneity and a willingness to interact with your audience. Do not approach these two methods of communicating the same way or use them for the same purposes.

The written medium is best used to inform. When you have a lot of facts and information to transfer to others, put it in writing. People can read five times faster than you can speak. Writing often activates rational thinking, the logical part of our minds. This is one of the reasons why reading from a written speech is so ineffective. Speaking is more than a mere transfer of data.

When you **want to persuade — to move people to action and to reach them emotionally – speak to them.** With spoken communication, people take in information with many of their senses. Listeners are affected by the emotion you convey, your tone and nuance, gestures and volume, and hundreds of other stimuli unavailable in the written word.

With The Decker Grid System®, you will never again have to write out a speech, word by laborious word. You will never again drone on and on in a three-minute voicemail. Your input at a meeting will be heard and, at the very least, considered for action.

Use trigger words. When you prepare a spoken message, don't write out sentences. It is far more efficient to create with building blocks, each one made up of the concepts and ideas you wish to communicate. These building blocks, or trigger words, serve as a prompt to the wealth of working knowledge within your mind. You can think of them as file names or key words within files.

Definition: The shortest word, group of words, or symbols about which you could talk for thirty seconds to five minutes.

weight
loss
Enc

EXAMPLE:

SUBJECT: WHY TAKE UP RUNNING?

The following are trigger words to quickly jog the author's mind for a speech about running. Note that they are short and many would make sense only to the author. Seeing each word brings forth more information related to that word.

Trigger words enable you to quickly and easily capture and organize large quantities of information. They simply act as file names that access the detail in the powerful computer called your brain.

weight loss

endorphins

fitness

Fitness

orphins

Assemble your tools. The Decker Grid System® consists of:
- Message Folders
- **Post-it® Notes**
- Success Guide

THE DECKER GRID SYSTEM® MESSAGE FOLDERS

These folders are enormously useful for walking you through the process of:
- Laying the Cornerstones
- Creating ideas
- Clustering ideas into themes
- Composing a message that motivates
- Communicating your completed message

The inside of a Message Folder is shown on pages 14 and 15. There is a Message Folder in the back pocket of this Success Guide for use in creating your message. The last page of this guide provides information on how you can purchase additional folders.

The left-hand page of the Message Folder assists you with the first three steps. The fourth step, called the Compose step, uses the right-hand page. We recommend your completed Message Folder serve as a reference when you actually communicate your message to your listener(s). It can then be filed and kept for future communications on the same subject.

Give us the tools, and we will finish the job. – Winston Churchill

POST-IT® NOTES

Post-it® Notes are the great 3M invention of little yellow pads of paper with adhesive on each piece. **Post-it® Notes** are the means by which you organize your ideas in The Decker Grid System®. Your trigger words conveniently fit onto the small size **Post-it® Notes** (one-and-one-half by two inches), which in turn, fit into the squares on the Message Folder.

Post-it® Notes are made to be mobile. Not every idea that occurs to you will be used. The ones that are used could end up in any order. The mobility of **Post-it® Notes** allows you to shuffle ideas around quickly, sorting and discarding them as if you were playing cards, until you finally arrange them for maximum clarity and impact. The Decker Grid System® prompts you through this activity so that, in no time flat, you achieve order from chaos.

Important note: We have found that **Post-it® Notes** work best in this exercise if you position them with the adhesive at the bottom before you write. This enables the note to curl up, making the trigger words easier to read.

SUCCESS GUIDE

This is your user's manual for The Decker Grid System®. This Guide is designed to walk you through the process step-by-step. We encourage you to read it thoroughly the first time and then use it as a reference while you become more adept at using the system.

EXAMPLE: Here's an inside look at a Message Folder

1. CORNERSTONES

POINT OF VIEW (POV)

What is your feeling, opinion, attitude about the subject?

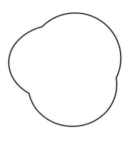

SUBJECT

BENEFITS

List three benefits
What benefits will your listeners receive from taking your Action Steps?

2. CREATE

Brainstorm for ideas.
Do not censor during this step!

3. CLUSTER

Arrange your ideas into natural groupings by find-ing common themes.
Title each cluster.

LISTENERS

Listener DNA
(Demographics, Needs/Interests, Attitudes)

1. Who are they?
2. What do they need/want to know about the subject?
3. How do they feel about the subject?

ACTION STEP(S)

List two action steps
1. What is the general action you want your listeners to take?
2. What is the specific action you want your listeners to take?
   (Make sure this action step is realistic, measurable, and includes a timeframe)

4. COMPOSE

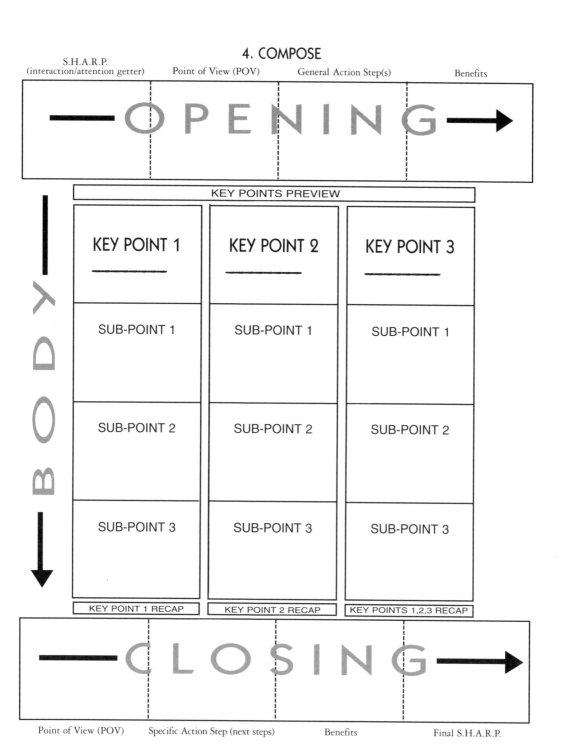

S.H.A.R.P.
(interaction/attention getter)

Point of View (POV)

General Action Step(s)

Benefits

OPENING →

KEY POINTS PREVIEW

BODY

KEY POINT 1	KEY POINT 2	KEY POINT 3
SUB-POINT 1	SUB-POINT 1	SUB-POINT 1
SUB-POINT 2	SUB-POINT 2	SUB-POINT 2
SUB-POINT 3	SUB-POINT 3	SUB-POINT 3
KEY POINT 1 RECAP	KEY POINT 2 RECAP	KEY POINTS 1,2,3 RECAP

CLOSING →

Point of View (POV)

Specific Action Step (next steps)

Benefits

Final S.H.A.R.P.

CREATING MESSAGES THAT MOTIVATE IS A FOUR-STEP PROCESS

Each step of The Decker Grid System® builds upon the one preceding it.

1 When you lay your Cornerstones, you create the context for your message. The Cornerstones establish the purpose, or foundation. They stimulate your thinking and focus your attention on your listener's perspective, what you want your listener to do, and how he/she will benefit.

2 When you Create, you unleash your mind's potential to generate ideas to support your subject.

3 When you Cluster, you naturally group your ideas according to common themes.

4 When you Compose, you organize and edit your clusters. The end result is your best ideas, arranged and ready to be communicated.

THE SKILL TO DO COMES FROM DOING

To experience the many benefits of this marvelous system, you need to begin to internalize the following four simple steps. Commit now to practicing each step as you read each section and review the example we provide.

TO DO: Think of a communication situation you have coming up in the next few days. It should be a situation where you will be communicating with others to inspire them to do something. It could be a subject at your next staff meeting, a discussion with your spouse about vacation plans, or a favor you need to ask from a friend. Use this same situation as you practice each of the steps in the process. By the end of this Success Guide, you will have developed your message to motivate your listeners to action. The work you do now will dramatically increase your effectiveness. We guarantee it!

Let's begin by laying the Cornerstones...

STEP ONE

Lay the Cornerstones For Success. What are you
going to talk about? Write your subject in the form of a trigger word or two
on a **Post-it® Note.** Open your Message Folder and place this **Post-it® Note**
on the upper center of the left page in the cloud labeled "SUBJECT." Note
that the cloud is rounded with no hard corners. This symbolizes the problem
with most subjects — they are too vague with no boundaries to give context
and focus to your ideas. The four Cornerstones are designed to solve that
problem by providing the context for your communication about your subject.

SUBJECT

EXAMPLE:

To help you understand each step in this process, I am going to create a scenario and use it all the way through. As you work on creating your own message that motivates, reference my example for clarity on how these steps take form.

Let's imagine that I live in a small city of 60,000 people. Recently, this small, quaint community has grown rapidly. In fact, the population has increased 20% in the last three years. I like to ride my bike and run in the parks. I've begun to notice a lot of trash in the parks and on the city streets. This was never a problem in previous years. I've decided to approach City Council with a proposal to begin to clean up our city.

The subject, then, of my message to be delivered to City Council in trigger words is...

CORNERSTONE ONE: THE ABC's OF POV

Your Point of View is your emotional connection to your subject. It is what brings life to the ideas you communicate.

Determine your Point of View (POV). Capture the feeling, attitude, or opinion you have about your subject in a few trigger words and write them on a **Post-it® Note**. Put it in the middle of the POV square (upper left side of the Message Folder surface). To make sure it meets the definition of POV, ask yourself these questions:

A. How do I really feel about my subject?
B. Why am I going to speak about this subject?
C. In my opinion, what is the current state of affairs regarding my subject?

Your POV should reflect your attitude about the subject. It should remain consistent, regardless of the listener, and create a sense of commitment or personal stake. Remember:

PEOPLE BUY ON Emotion & JUSTIFY WITH FACT.

EXAMPLE:

In my scenario, I would summarize my feeling, attitude, or opinion as follows: I feel a formal Clean Up Day is essential to cleaning up our city. It will help get trash off the streets and raise the community's awareness about the importance of a clean community throughout the entire year. The trigger words would look like this:

POINT OF VIEW (POV)

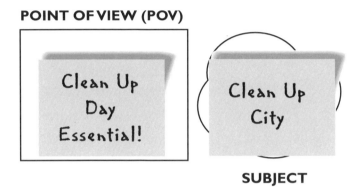

SUBJECT

KEYS TO REMEMBER...

- Your POV answers the "so what?" for your listeners about your subject
- It gets you in touch with how you feel regarding your subject
- Ultimately, your goal should be to have your listeners walk away sharing your POV on your subject

CORNERSTONE TWO: LISTENERS

Walk a mile in their shoes. Successful communicators demonstrate an understanding of their listener. Spend some time thinking about your subject from your listener's perspective. Generate information in each of these three areas:

- **D**emographics – (age, occupation, responsibility)
- **N**eeds and interests including current knowledge of your subject
- **A**ttitudes regarding you, your organization, your subject, and your POV

One easy way to remember these elements is to think of DNA (remember back to your high school biology class). You need to be clear as to who your listeners are, so spend time identifying their DNA. Just as DNA represents the genetic makeup of a person, so too, DNA in the listener profile identifies the makeup or characteristics of your listeners.

Make your information specific. Write trigger words to summarize your listeners' DNA on **Post-it® Notes**. Place them in the lower left-hand box on the Message Folder surface. It is absolutely essential to think about your listeners before you begin to create your message. Communicating from their perspective will enable you to be relevant. It will be what keeps their attention and helps move them to action.

If you don't know much about your listeners, take the time to find out what you can. Call a sample of them or talk to other people who know them.

P.S. Once you begin to identify your listeners, you may find you have several diverse groups within your large audience. If so, you will need to identify ways to address each of their needs or concerns in one message or deliver a tailored message to each group separately.

EXAMPLE:

Some of what I know about my listeners comes from direct personal contact and some from what I hear from others. Also, the local newspaper has given me some understanding of the Council and its goals.

The City Council is made up of our Mayor and Council members.

Demographics:	• all are long-term residents (> 5 years) • ages range from 35-60 • 60% men/40% women
Needs and interests:	• they want to improve the town by increasing business and furthering the sense of community • they have a desire to make some permanent contributions to our city's success
Attitudes:	• at least two of the members are very pro-environment and actively promote recycling

KEYS TO REMEMBER...
• Focus on your listeners
• Understand their DNA
• If you don't know much about your listeners, take the time to find out more
• Check in with listeners during your communication to ensure your information is accurate

Have I reached the person to whom I am speaking?
- Lily Tomlin as "Ernestine"

EXAMPLE:

1. CORNERSTONES

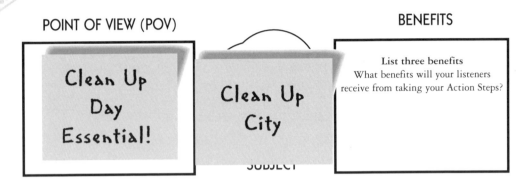

POINT OF VIEW (POV)

Clean Up
Day
Essential!

Clean Up
City

SUBJECT

BENEFITS

List three benefits
What benefits will your listeners
receive from taking your Action Steps?

2. CREATE

Brainstorm for ideas.
Do not censor during this
step!

3. CLUSTER

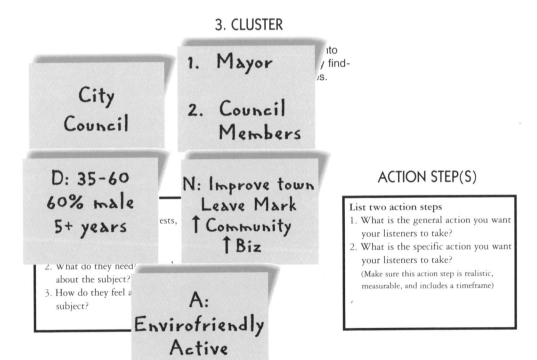

City
Council

1. Mayor

2. Council
Members

D: 35-60
60% male
5+ years

N: Improve town
Leave Mark
↑ Community
↑ Biz

ests,

2. What do they need
about the subject?
3. How do they feel a
subject?

A:
Envirofriendly
Active

ACTION STEP(S)

List two action steps
1. What is the general action you want
   your listeners to take?
2. What is the specific action you want
   your listeners to take?
   (Make sure this action step is realistic,
   measurable, and includes a timeframe)

CORNERSTONE THREE: ACTION STEPS - SHOW THEM THE WAY.

Decide what you want your listeners to do with your message. In the process of communicating to them, help them understand where you want to go with your idea. By being clear and specific with your Action Steps, you are telling them how they can help you succeed.

Choose a General Action and Specific Actions. Write each of them down on a **Post-it® Note** and place them in the lower right square on the Message Folder surface.

The General Action is the "big" action that reflects what you would like your audience to do, or feel, or perhaps even be, in broad terms. The Specific Actions should be measurable, realistic, and timebound. Clearly defined Specific Actions will give your listeners ways to demonstrate their empathy or agreement with your POV.

By determining Action Steps before you create your message, you will focus your mind on your desired outcomes and the resulting message will reflect them.

EXAMPLE:

I would like the City Council to consider the merits of my proposal. More specifically, I would like them to:

- Dedicate the first Saturday in June as "Clean Up Day"
- Promote the event prior to June and then actively participate in it

GENERAL ACTION   **SPECIFIC ACTIONS**

Consider Proposal

Dedicate 1st Sat. June

Promote Participate

KEYS TO REMEMBER...

General Action guidelines:

- Be general
- Describe the big action you want listeners to take
- Examples – be open, consider the possibility...

Specific Action guidelines:

- Be specific
- Make it measurable
- Be realistic
- Set a time frame

EXAMPLE:

1. CORNERSTONES

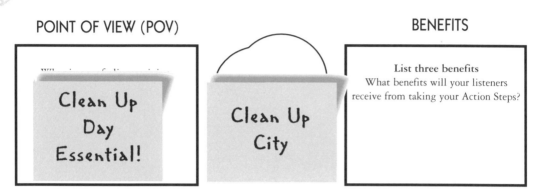

POINT OF VIEW (POV)

Clean Up
Day
Essential!

Clean Up
City

BENEFITS

List three benefits
What benefits will your listeners
receive from taking your Action Steps?

2. CREATE

Brainstorm for ideas.
Do not censor during this
step!

3. CLUSTER

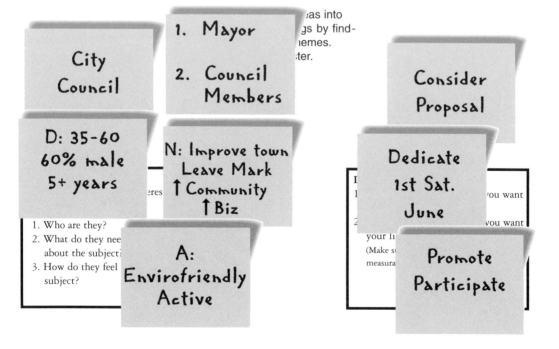

City
Council

1. Mayor

2. Council
Members

Consider
Proposal

D: 35-60
60% male
5+ years

N: Improve town
Leave Mark
↑ Community
↑ Biz

Dedicate
1st Sat.
June

1. Who are they?
2. What do they nee
   about the subject?
3. How do they feel
   subject?

A:
Envirofriendly
Active

Promote
Participate

CORNERSTONE FOUR: BENEFITS

Tell them the WIIFM. That is, "what's in it for **me**?" – "me" being your listeners. Identify what personal benefits your listeners will receive from taking your Action Steps. If each listener is agreeable to your POV and taking those actions, how will he or she be better off?

Avoid generic business benefits. Identify three benefits that satisfy the needs and interests of your listeners. To help you generate ideas, re-read your trigger words in your Action Step and Listener Cornerstones.

Write each Benefit (trigger words) on a separate **Post-it® Note**. Place the Benefit **Post-it® Notes** in the box in the upper right corner of the Message Folder, listing them in order of importance.

EXAMPLE:

If the City Council considers my proposal, dedicates the first Saturday in June as Clean Up Day, promotes it, and participates, they will realize the following benefits:

- citizen appreciation
- a cleaner city
- a permanent contribution to the city's future success

I believe these benefits will be important to my City Council based on what I know about them as described by my Listener Cornerstone.

KEYS TO REMEMBER...

- Benefits must be specific to your listeners, based on their needs and interests

- Benefits will result from taking your suggested actions

- Avoid generic benefits wherever possible

EXAMPLE:

1. CORNERSTONES

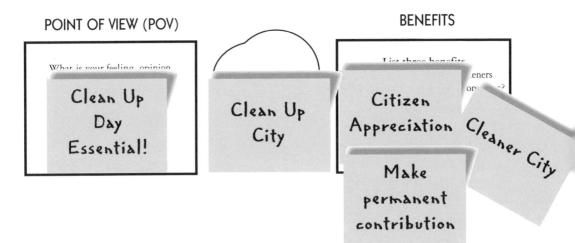

POINT OF VIEW (POV)

What is your feeling, opinion...

Clean Up
Day
Essential!

Clean Up
City

BENEFITS

List three benefits...
...eners
on...

Citizen
Appreciation

Cleaner City

Make
permanent
contribution

2. CREATE

Brainstorm for ideas.
Do not censor during this
step!

3. CLUSTER

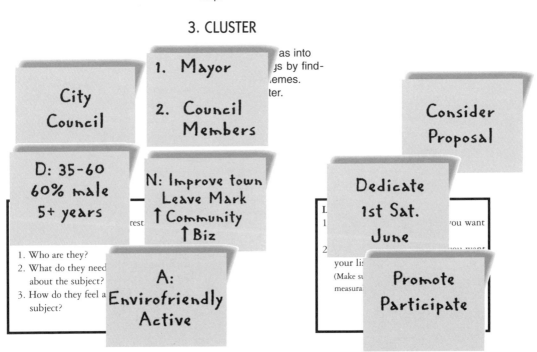

...as into
...gs by find-
...emes.
...ter.

City
Council

1. Mayor

2. Council
Members

Consider
Proposal

D: 35-60
60% male
5+ years

N: Improve town
Leave Mark
↑ Community
↑ Biz

Dedicate
1st Sat.
June

1. Who are they?
2. What do they need
   about the subject?
3. How do they feel a
   subject?

A:
Envirofriendly
Active

1
2
your lis
(Make su
measura

you want

Promote
Participate

STEP TWO

It's time to CREATE. The CREATE step is analogous to doing a mental search and retrieval of anything that pops into your consciousness when you think of your subject. This is the time to brainstorm. Let your ideas flow in a rapid stream, uninterrupted by the tendency to prematurely organize. The result of a successful brainstorm is a deluge of facts, figures, stories, background, personal experiences, and case histories. New perceptions and ideas will occur to you during brainstorming that you would have missed in a more traditional process, such as writing from an outline.

It is essential to remember that order comes <u>after</u> chaos. This is the principal reason why The Decker Grid System® is so effective. We are usually taught to create and organize at the **same** time. Our minds don't work that way.

To begin the creative process, place the Message Folder beside you. Focus your attention on the left–hand page. Your Cornerstone **Post-it® Notes** are already in place, establishing the context for your message. Your mind is now focused on what you want to accomplish. Create some blank space in front of you, ready to be filled with the wealth of your thoughts, images, stories, facts, and other ideas. You will now get those ideas out by writing trigger words on **Post-it® Notes**. One idea per **Post-it® Note**. Generate your **Post-it® Notes** as quickly as possible, sticking them anywhere in the open space in front of you. Remember, logical sequencing comes in the next step, after you CREATE.

EXAMPLE:

After reviewing my Cornerstones, I spent five minutes jotting down trigger words for every idea that came to me. The results are as follows:

Aerobics
Warmup
Mayor

Trashbags
in Nsp

Promotion

↑ Pop
20%

Garbage ↑

Day to ↑
Consciousness

City
quadrants

Radio/
TV

Washington
Park
start - end

Trash
Parks
Streets

BFI Truck
Sponsor

BBQ
After

Volunteer
Orgs

Activate!

Hertz
Rent A
Car

Power of
Community

teams

TO DO:

1   Set a timer for five minutes. Try to brainstorm at least fifteen new ideas on **Post-it® Notes** on a clear space in front of you.

2   Write down any facts, ideas, concepts, details, case histories, examples, etc., that occur to you on your subject. Include stories, quotes and analogies. Do <u>not</u> censor!

3   Use trigger words or symbols.

4   Don't worry about sticking the **Post-it® Notes** in any kind of order. Avoid over-thinking or "wordsmithing."

5   Ready. Set. Go!

KEYS TO REMEMBER...

• Set a time limit: five minutes to start with

• Do not censor any ideas

• Go for quantity, not quality

STEP THREE

Cluster Like *Crazy!* The Cluster step creates order from your brainstorming. It is based on identifying the natural groupings that flow from the ideas you generated during the Create step. Clustering is the process of surveying your brainstorm results and identifying natural categories.

You now have ten to twenty randomly placed **Post-it® Notes** from the **Create** step filling the surface in front of you. The object is to find the common themes.

When you have placed all of your ideas in clusters, the final part of this step is to assign a label to each cluster. On another **Post-it® Note**, write the title of the label and place it at the top of the cluster. The label should best capture the concept that the cluster addresses. Use trigger words for your labels and underline each one to distinguish it from the others in the cluster.

Your labels will become the KEY POINTS in your message. The **Post-it® Notes** that make up each cluster become your SUB-POINTS. At this stage, you might have three to six clusters - each with anywhere from one to ten Sub-points within the cluster.

EXAMPLE:

Why a
Clean up day?

Trash
Parks
Streets

Power of
Community

↑ Pop
20%

Day to ↑
Consciousness

Garbage ↑

Activate!

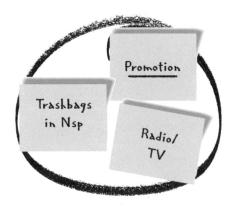

Promotion

Trashbags
in Nsp

Radio/
TV

Day's
Agenda

Washington
Park
start - end

BBQ
After

City
quadrants

Aerobics
Warmup
Mayor

teams

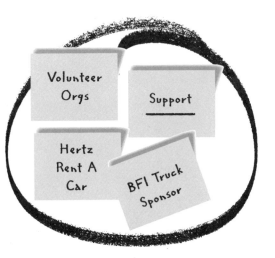

Volunteer
Orgs

Support

Hertz
Rent A
Car

BFI Truck
Sponsor

TO DO:

1   Pick one **Post-it® Note** (idea) and place it in the open space in front of you. Then find another idea that is similar to it and move it to that area. Add any other ideas common to that group to form a cluster.

2   Continue to move the **Post-it® Notes** around to make clusters. They should be natural groupings that address or elaborate on the same point. Do not force all **Post-it® Notes** into clusters.

3   When you have placed your ideas in clusters, assign a label or title to each cluster. Write the label down on another **Post-it® Note**, underline it, and place it at the top of the cluster.

4   Review each cluster and brainstorm for additional ideas. Review your Cornerstones to help stimulate your thinking. If ideas occur, capture them on **Post-it® Notes** and add them to the appropriate cluster.

KEYS TO REMEMBER...

- Find similarities between **Post-it® Notes** and group them together
- Clusters can have anywhere from two to ten **Post-it® Notes**
- Assign a label to describe each cluster, write it on a **Post-it® Note**, and underline it
- Review each cluster and brainstorm for additional ideas
- Labels will become KEY POINTS
- The **Post-it® Notes** within each cluster become SUB-POINTS

STEP FOUR

Compose your Masterpiece. The Compose step is the final organizing and editing of your ideas. You want to be left with only your best ideas to communicate. You will compose the Body of your message before you work on your Opening and Closing.

Begin with the Body. Keep it simple. People remember the main points that are said, not all of the detail. Use the "Rule of Three" as your guide. Three key points is a proven standard of simplicity, and this discipline will help you avoid a pitfall of many communicators called "data dump." Dumping loads of information on hapless listeners is counterproductive since short-term memory is, indeed, short.

On the right-hand page of your Message Folder there is a layout for your final message. Notice the places to put your three best Key Points in the appropriate boxes at the top of each column. The best three Sub-points from the cluster will then be moved under the corresponding Key Point.

When finished composing the Body, you will probably have several extra **Post-it® Notes** remaining that have not yet been used. You may want to review them to see if any of these ideas are better than those currently being used. You will often find that a Key Point from an unused cluster will make a better Sub-point than one already chosen. You may also re-write **Post-it® Notes**, using broader terms to consolidate several overly-detailed ones.

EXAMPLE:

Looking back at the four clusters I've created, I will begin my work with Why a clean up day? Let's look at the cluster before and after I work through the Compose step....

KEY POINT ONE

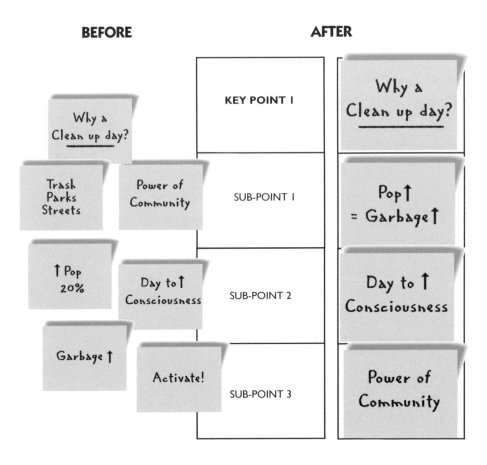

BEFORE   **AFTER**

I've consolidated two **Post-it® Notes** into one and eliminated two altogether. Let's look now at Support and Promotion....

EXAMPLE:

In this case, I've combined two clusters into one and reworded **Post-it®**
Notes to make them more general. BFI/Truck Sponsor and Hertz Rent-A-Car
were combined to become Corporate Sponsors. Trashbags in newspaper and
Radio/TV became one **Post-it® Note** as well.

KEY POINT TWO

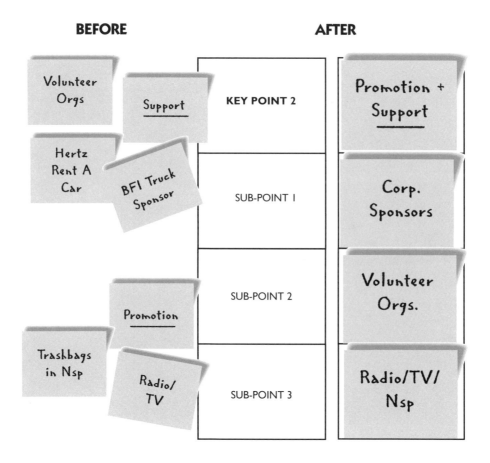

BEFORE   **AFTER**

Volunteer Orgs

Support

KEY POINT 2

Promotion + Support

Hertz Rent A Car

BFI Truck Sponsor

SUB-POINT 1

Corp. Sponsors

Promotion

SUB-POINT 2

Volunteer Orgs.

Trashbags in Nsp

Radio/ TV

SUB-POINT 3

Radio/TV/ Nsp

EXAMPLE:

The BBQ and Recycle Fair were combined and put as the last Sub-point because they will finish off the day. Teams and city quadrants were combined. Aerobics warmup by Mayor will be used a little later in the section on Attention Getters and Memory Hooks...

KEY POINT THREE

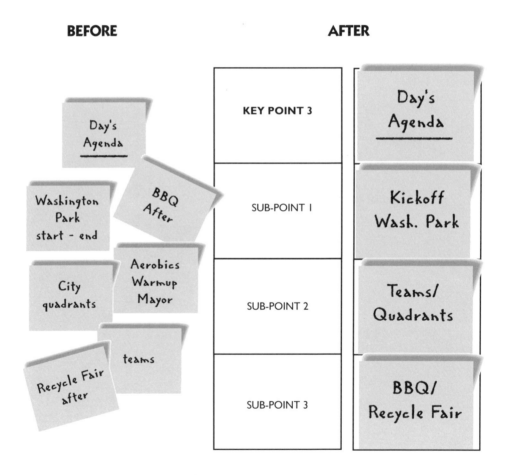

BEFORE	AFTER

TO DO:

1 With the Message Folder placed open, select the three most important Key Points (or labels) from your clusters. Prioritize them, placing the **Post-it®** **Notes** in the appropriate Key Point boxes. Often Key Point #1 will be introductory (the background or the current state) building to Key Point #3, the most important. Your sequence may be different – arrange them for maximum impact.

2 Review all the Sub-points in the Key Point #1 cluster, pick the best three, and prioritize them. Place these ordered Sub-point **Post-it® Notes** in the first column on the right side of your Message Folder.

3 Repeat the above process in #2 for the remaining Key Points and selected Sub-points.

4 Look at your unused **Post-it® Notes** to see if there are any that are better than the ones you've selected. Feel free to mix and match at this stage to capture all of your best ideas.

5 Do any re-writing that is necessary.

KEYS TO REMEMBER...

• Compose the Body first

• Remember The Rule of Three

• Look for the best ideas and ways to consolidate multiple **Post-it® Notes** into one

Composing the Opening. There are many ways to begin your message. The basic Opening outlined here will serve as a standard that is quick to create and highly effective. It will provide a road map of where you are going, and will let your listeners know the benefits resulting from taking the trip. You simply state your POV, General Action, and a summarized Benefit Statement. Later on, you will learn ways to add an effective Attention Getter in the Opening, but for now let's leave that space blank.

The beginning is the most important part of the work. – Plato

EXAMPLE:

4. COMPOSE

S.H.A.R.P. (interaction/attention getter)	Point of View (POV)	General Action Step(s)	Benefits
	Clean Up Day Essential!	Consider Proposal	Appreciation Cleaner City Perm. Contribution

→ O P E N I N G →

TO DO:

1 Return to the Cornerstones on the left side of your Message Folder. Most of the **Post-it® Notes** from your Cornerstones will still be in place. If you used some in the Body of your message, re-create them for use in your Opening.

2 There is space for four **Post-it® Notes** in the Opening section of the Message Folder. For now, leave the first Attention Getter box empty and place your POV **Post-it® Note** next to it, as indicated. Your POV tells your listeners how you feel about your subject.

3 Place the General Action **Post-it® Note** in the middle of the Opening panel. You will tell them what you want them to do in broad general terms.

4 Re-write your best benefits onto one **Post-it® Note**. Place this Benefit **Post-it® Note** on the right side of the Opening panel. You will complete your Opening by telling your listeners what's in it for them. By communicating the benefits right up front, you give your listeners a reason for listening.

KEYS TO REMEMBER...

• A good opening is critical to setting the context for your message

• State your POV

• State your General Action Step

• Give a summary of Benefits to listeners for taking your desired action

Composing the Closing. There are many ways to finish a message. The basic Closing outlined here is easy to create and effective when delivered. It will reinforce your ideas and commit you to leaving your listeners on a positive note. Later in the next section, we will add a Memory Hook to the Closing; for now, let's just leave it blank.

You will simply restate your POV, tell your listeners the Specific Action(s) you want them to take (rather than the General Action used in the Opening), and leave your listeners by re-stating the Benefits they will receive from taking your desired actions.

As a final check, review your Listener Cornerstone, followed by POV, Actions, and Benefits. Then read over your Message Opening, Body, and Closing.

EXAMPLE:

I need to re-write my POV and summary Benefit **Post-it® Notes** to include in my Closing. I will take my Specific Actions and combine them on one **Post-it® Note** for my Closing.

Clean Up Day Essential!	Dedicate 1st Sat. in June Promote + Participate	Appreciation Cleaner City Perm. Contribution	
Point of View (POV)	Specific Action Step (next steps)	Benefits	Final S.H.A.R.P.

TO DO:

1 There is space for four **Post-it® Notes** in the Closing section of the Message Folder. On a new **Post-it® Note**, write the POV from your Opening, and place it on the left side of the Closing panel.

2 Returning to the Action Step Cornerstone from your Message Folder, place the Specific Action Steps in the middle of the Closing panel. (Whereas you will give your listeners the General Action Step in your Opening, giving them the Specific Actions in your Closing will sharpen their focus on exactly what you want them to do.) If you have more than one, consolidate them onto one **Post-it® Note**.

3 On a new **Post-it® Note**, write the summary of Benefits used in your Opening and place it on the right side of the Closing panel. Your last statement is your most memorable one. End your presentation by repeating the benefits to listeners of sharing your POV and taking your desired actions.

KEYS TO REMEMBER...

It's time to review the final checklist and make appropriate adjustments.
Have you:

- stated your position and feeling (POV) on the subject? ☐

- addressed the needs and interests of your audience? ☐

- clearly communicated the actions you want your listeners to take within a certain time frame? ☐

- included the benefits they will receive by taking these actions? ☐

If you answered no to any of these questions, you need to modify one or more **Post-it® Notes**.

EXAMPLE:

1. CORNERSTONES

POINT OF VIEW (POV)

What is your feeling, opinion

**Clean Up
Day
Essential!**

**Clean Up
City**

BENEFITS

List three benefits

...eners

on ...?

**Citizen
Appreciation**

Cleaner City

**Make
permanent
contribution**

2. CREATE

Brainstorm for ideas.
Do not censor during this
step!

3. CLUSTER

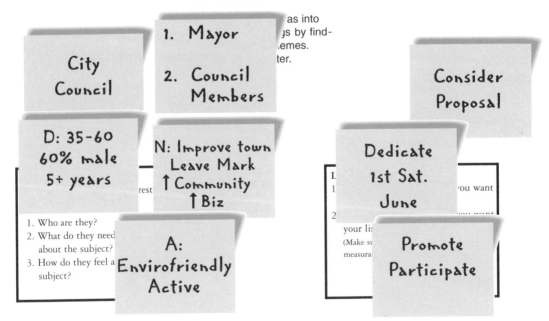

as into
gs by find-
...emes.
...ter.

1. Mayor

**2. Council
Members**

**City
Council**

**Consider
Proposal**

**D: 35-60
60% male
5+ years**

**N: Improve town
Leave Mark
↑ Community
↑ Biz**

**Dedicate
1st Sat.
June**

1. Who are they?
2. What do they need
   about the subject?
3. How do they feel a
   subject?

rest

**A:
Envirofriendly
Active**

L
1
2
your lis
(Make s
measura

you want

**Promote
Participate**

4. COMPOSE

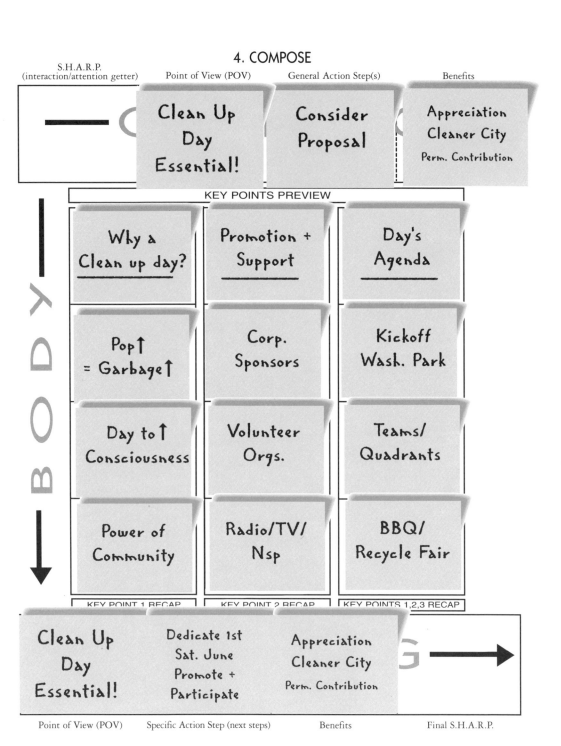

S.H.A.R.P.
(interaction/attention getter)

Point of View (POV)

General Action Step(s)

Benefits

Clean Up Day Essential!

Consider Proposal

Appreciation Cleaner City Perm. Contribution

KEY POINTS PREVIEW

Why a Clean up day?

Promotion + Support

Day's Agenda

Pop↑ = Garbage↑

Corp. Sponsors

Kickoff Wash. Park

Day to↑ Consciousness

Volunteer Orgs.

Teams/ Quadrants

Power of Community

Radio/TV/ Nsp

BBQ/ Recycle Fair

KEY POINT 1 RECAP   KEY POINT 2 RECAP   KEY POINTS 1,2,3 RECAP

Clean Up Day Essential!

Dedicate 1st Sat. June Promote + Participate

Appreciation Cleaner City Perm. Contribution

Point of View (POV)

Specific Action Step (next steps)

Benefits

Final S.H.A.R.P.

BODY

ATTENTION GETTERS & MEMORY HOOKS

Research has established that listeners more easily remember the first and last comments made in a discussion or presentation than the stuff in-between. Therefore, it is critically important that you are effective in getting listener attention at the onset to increase the desire to pay attention to the body of your message. And, that you provide a memorable closing statement that motivates them to take your desired action.

> **The key to obtaining and maintaining listener attention is the use of images and emotion created by language or visual support. The human mind loves images and emotion.**

Why do our listeners need help listening and remembering? Because they have a chronic case of information overload. That, coupled with an average adult attention span of eight seconds, means communicators have their work cut out for them!

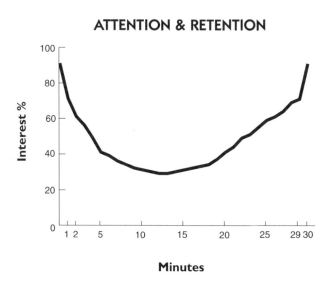

ATTENTION & RETENTION

Source: Effective Business and Technical Presentations, 3rd edition • George L. Morrisey and Thomas L. Sechrest

At Decker Communications we have identified five principles that will enable you to capture audience attention, emphasize what is important in your information, and boost listener retention of your Key Points. We call them the S.H.A.R.P. principles:

S - **Stories and Examples**
H - **Humor**
A - **Analogies**
R - **References and Quotes**
P - **Pictures/Visual Aids**

These S.H.A.R.P. principles should be used strategically and consciously in your communications. You need to identify one or two of these principles that work best for you naturally.

STORIES AND EXAMPLES

For thousands of centuries stories have been a highly effective method of communicating ideas. We all have personal experiences or know of others' experiences that can add "humanness," depth, and emotion to our messages. Real–life experiences are the easiest to remember and use. Even hypothetical examples, allegories, and fairytales can be effective in making ideas more memorable.

Your story or example can be either directly or indirectly related to your topic. When it is indirectly related, you need to work harder at making the link between it and your subject in the minds of your listeners by clearly stating the connection.

EXAMPLE:

Back to my Clean Up Day scenario, a story comes to mind of a recent experience in which I was running in the park. A teenager in front of me opened a candy bar and threw the wrapper on the ground. I stopped, picked up the paper, handed it back to him and said, "The trash can is just over there." He proceeded to walk over and drop it in the can. He seemed to need that reminder. To remember my story, I will create the following **Post-it® Note**:

Teenager
Candy

TO DO:

Take the time now to think about a story or example that would apply to your message. Use trigger words to write it on a **Post-it® Note** and put it to the side. We will add it to your message a little later.

KEYS TO REMEMBER...

- Be brief – 30 seconds to 1 minute maximum

- Use sensory language to build word pictures in the minds of listeners

- Tell the story as you would tell it sitting around the dinner table

- After the story or example, state the point explicitly and relate it back to your Point of View or Key Point

HUMOR

Incorporating humor into your message is not about telling jokes. Instead, it is about adding lightness and personality to your message. Humor, properly used, helps bring energy to the people in the room and subconsciously reminds us of our uniquely human condition. The other big benefit of humor is that it helps to improve the communicator's delivery because it tends to increase one's level of comfort and relaxation.

TO DO:

Take the time now to think about where you might add a little humor to your message. Write it down on a **Post-it® Note** using trigger words and put it off to the side, next to your Story or Example.

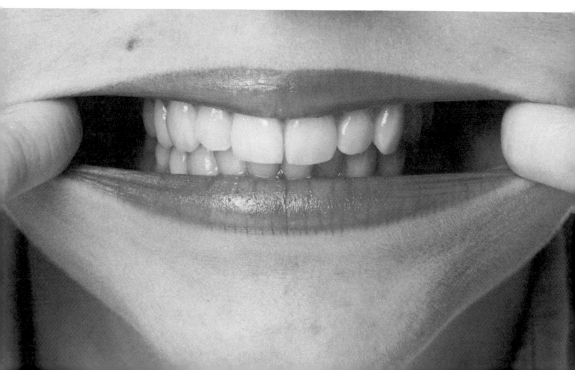

EXAMPLE:

In my Clean Up Day example, I was thinking about the Kickoff in Washington Park and an image came to mind. The Mayor was leading an aerobics warm-up for all volunteers. If I can paint the word picture of the fun we could all have, it will add humor to my message. Here's my **Post-it® Note**:

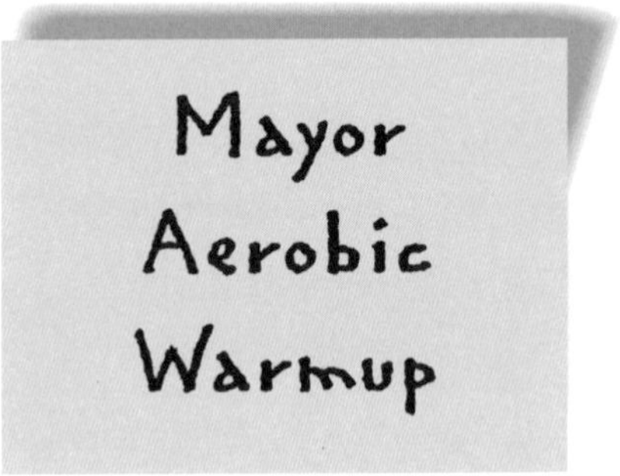

Mayor
Aerobic
Warmup

KEYS TO REMEMBER...

• Attitude – Let the lightness flow naturally
• Don't be disappointed if your effort does not produce
  belly laughs. The intent is to add positive energy,
  not to be labeled a comedian
• Balance humor with seriousness. Use humor strategically to draw
  attention to a particular point that is necessary to the core of your message
• Exaggerate elements of your content to humorous proportions

ANALOGIES

It is a natural function of the human mind to compare, contrast, categorize, and cross-reference. This function is what creates analogies.

To develop an analogy, ask yourself how your object, process, or concept is like something else. The similarities could be physical, emotional, or functional. Then write two or three trigger words on a **Post-it® Note** to identify the analogy and put it off to the side, next to your Humor and Story **Post-it® Notes**.

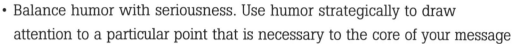

Analogies not only help with listener interest and memorability, they can also simplify a complex concept.

EXAMPLE:

The concept of a community of people assembling for a Clean Up Day reminds me of the stories I've heard from my parents about a Barn Raising. They've told me of families coming from miles around to work from morning until night on getting a barn built and raised. I could talk about the power of bringing people together to achieve a common goal using this barn raising analogy.

Barn
Raising

TO DO:

What analogy could you use in your message? Think of something similar to one of your Key Points or Sub-points and write it on a **Post-it® Note**. Place it with the other S.H.A.R.P. **Post-it® Notes** which we will add to our message soon.

KEYS TO REMEMBER...

• One analogy per concept; otherwise, you diminish the effect

• You must build the imagery around the link between the two ideas you are comparing. It is not enough to allude to things that have similarity; to be effective, you need to spend the time necessary to describe why and how the two items are similar

• Vary the type of analogies you use. Don't just use analogies from sports or history. Be sensitive to your Listener Cornerstone in identifying analogous subjects that would make sense to your listeners based on their DNA

• Choose analogies that have a positive emotional context

REFERENCES AND QUOTES

A reference is any independent source of information that you cite to support your points. It can be something someone once did, an excerpt from an industry or trade journal, an article in a newspaper, or a program on radio or television.

A quote is re-stating what someone else once said. It can be a formal quote from a book or article, an informal quote such as something your mother always said, a slogan that a company is using in an ad campaign, or lyrics from a song. Your local bookstore carries a section of quotation books on various subjects. These books can be very handy when putting together your message that motivates.

EXAMPLE:

To support the increasing need for attention to a cleaner city, I would like to reference some statistics from City Hall on the increase in population of our city over the last few years and the resulting increase in trash. I called the garbage collection company and they provided some data on the increase in garbage trucks and tons of garbage going to the dump. In trigger words I will create a **Post-it® Note** as follows:

Stats on
pop. growth

TO DO:

Do you know of a quote that applies to your message? An article you read that was related to your topic? If so, add this **Post-it® Note** to your collection of S.H.A.R.P. **Post-it® Notes**.

KEYS TO REMEMBER...

Some helpful suggestions on using references and quotes:

• Read a quote rather than misquoting what someone said. Be sure to acknowledge the source if it is known

• Introduce the reference or quote to prepare the listener(s) to pay close attention to what is coming

• Select only the most powerful portions of a long reference or quote

• Don't read lengthy passages

• Don't leave this Attention Getter on its own – tie it back to your subject to ensure that its relevance is obvious

The man who can think and does not know how to express what he thinks is at the level of him who cannot think.

– Pericles

PICTURES/VISUAL AIDS

A spoken message, reinforced with a well-designed visual aid, has greater impact than one merely spoken or communicated solely with the visual aid.

Pictures and visual aids are important in helping an audience understand a concept. Complex data can be organized and reduced to a graphic, a chart, or a table to make a point clearly and concisely.

The most common problems with visual aids are: overuse, poor design and construction, and awkward transitions between the visual and the communicator.

THE FOLLOWING STATISTICS HELP TO COMMUNICATE THE POWER OF VISUAL SUPPORT:

- Retention increases from 14% to 38% when listeners see, as well as hear, a presentation.
- Presentations using visual aids were found to be 43% more persuasive than unaided presentations.
  - Group consensus is 21% higher in meetings in which visual aids are incorporated.
    - The time required to communicate a concept can be reduced up to 40% with the use of effective visuals.

source: 3M Meeting Management Institute

The media you choose will help determine the look and feel of your visual. Your choice for any given communication event can also be affected by the following:

- equipment/tools available
- environment in which you will be communicating
- number of listeners in the group
- type of content to be represented visually

Software programs like Microsoft® PowerPoint®, for designing and delivering visuals, have greatly increased the use of computer-based visuals in everything from one-on-ones, to small meetings, and presentations to hundreds. The benefits of computer-based visuals are: the range of color and graphics available; the flexibility to make last-minute changes; the ability to put forth a professional image; greater impact on the listeners.

Low-tech tools such as flip charts and pads of paper used in conversation can still be highly effective tools for complementing a communicator.

Some of the best visual aids we have seen in our work with over 100,000 professionals have been props. A ball of yarn and scissors, an apple, a box wrapped with a big, beautiful red ribbon.... These props are both simple and highly effective memory hooks for listeners. Be creative. Let your imagination run free!

EXAMPLE:

In my presentation to the City Council, I envision two opportunities for pictures/visual aids. The first use is in a dramatic opening in which I can show slides of the garbage that is now common in our parks and on our streets.

Also, in conjunction with the statistics on population and garbage growth, I can create a line graph as visual support to help demonstrate the increases over the last five years.

Garbage
Pictures

Line Chart
Pop +
Garbage↑

TO DO:

What visual aids could you use to help communicate your concepts? Take a piece of paper and sketch some ideas of what your visuals might look like. Write two or three descriptive words on a **Post-it® Note** and put it with your other S.H.A.R.P. **Post-it® Notes.**

KEYS TO REMEMBER...

When developing your visual aids, keep three things in mind:

BIG – make them large enough so that every listener can see them without squinting.

BOLD – use bright, contrasting colors. Use pictures instead of words wherever possible.

BASIC – the goal is not to overwhelm, but to simplify the complex. If your visual is complicated it will detract from the effectiveness of your message.

ADDING IN YOUR ATTENTION GETTERS AND MEMORY HOOKS

TO DO:

It is now time to add the Attention Getters and Memory Hooks to your message. Open up your Message Folder and look at the S.H.A.R.P. **Post-it®** **Notes** that you've created.

> **Which of them would help to get attention initially? Place this Post-it® Note at the very beginning of your Opening.**

Which of them would be most effective at powerfully reinforcing your message? This Memory Hook can become your final comment in your Closing.

The rest of your Attention Getters and Memory Hooks can be scattered sparingly throughout the body of your communication in places where they strategically complement a Key Point. Add the ones you feel will have the most impact. You can place them off to the side of your existing points, or replace a Sub-point with a S.H.A.R.P. if you feel it is more effective.

If you have some time between the preparation and delivery of your message, you may find even better S.H.A.R.P. examples which can be added and exchanged for your present ones.

EXAMPLE:

In evaluating the S.H.A.R.P. **Post-it® Notes** I've generated for my Clean Up message, I have selected and arranged them as follows:

EXAMPLE:

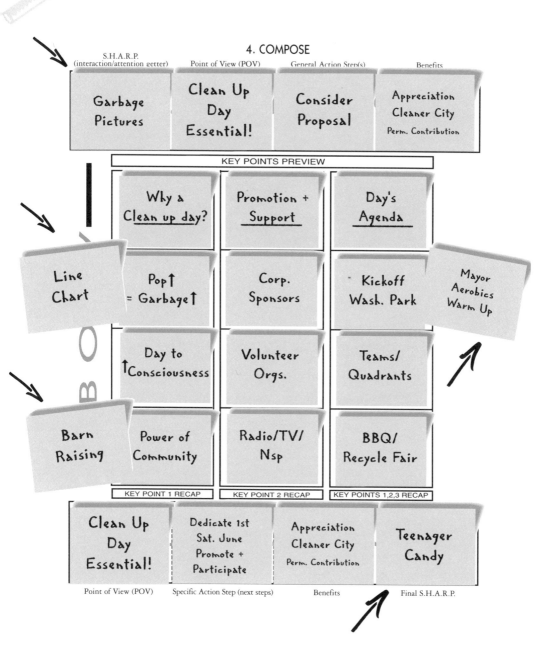

4. COMPOSE

S.H.A.R.P. (interaction/attention getter)	Point of View (POV)	General Action Step(s)	Benefits
Garbage Pictures	Clean Up Day Essential!	Consider Proposal	Appreciation Cleaner City Perm. Contribution

KEY POINTS PREVIEW

Why a Clean up day?	Promotion + Support	Day's Agenda

Line Chart	Pop↑ = Garbage↑	Corp. Sponsors	Kickoff Wash. Park	Mayor Aerobics Warm Up
	Day to ↑Consciousness	Volunteer Orgs.	Teams/ Quadrants	
Barn Raising	Power of Community	Radio/TV/ Nsp	BBQ/ Recycle Fair	

KEY POINT 1 RECAP	KEY POINT 2 RECAP	KEY POINTS 1,2,3 RECAP

Clean Up Day Essential!	Dedicate 1st Sat. June Promote + Participate	Appreciation Cleaner City Perm. Contribution	Teenager Candy
Point of View (POV)	Specific Action Step (next steps)	Benefits	Final S.H.A.R.P.

STEP FIVE

Enough Preparation – Now Speak! Now that you have created a message that will motivate your listeners to take action, it is time to deliver it. The delivery of your message is critically important to getting results.

> At Decker Communications, we focus on individuals building the necessary skills to:
>
> • establish trust and believability with their listeners
>
> • enhance their own natural communication style

We focus on these delivery skills to ensure a communicator's message is heard, understood, and acted upon.

- Sustaining eye communication to gain attention and build trust

- Maintaining strong posture and purposeful movement to communicate confidence and openness

- Using gestures and facial expression to reflect energy and attitude

- Using language and pauses to add clarity and emphasis

- Varying voice to reflect energy and emotion

- Ensuring appropriate dress and appearance to align with listeners

- Involving listeners to increase attention and retention

- Building on one's natural style to enhance trust and believability

If you feel that you can improve upon how you communicate your messages, take action. There are several ways to improve your skills. Seminars and private consultations are available from Decker Communications and others. There are also some excellent products available on the subject. We offer books, tapes and videos as tools. Practice and video feedback can be very helpful. Take every opportunity to get input from others and to see yourself in action. Use this information to modify your communication behavior to make it more effective.

TA DA - YOU'RE ON!

It's time to communicate with your listeners. Deliver your message in the following sequence:

Opening – start with your Attention Getter. Transition to your POV. Then state General Action and Summary of Benefits.

Preview your Key Points – state the Key Points that you will discuss in the Body of your presentation. This previews the structure of your message and enables listeners to follow your "Table of Contents." Your preview may begin with the words, "Today I will discuss...."

Body –

Address Key Point #1 – followed by its Sub-points

Address Key Point #2 – followed by its Sub-points

Address Key Point #3 – followed by its Sub-points

Do a Key Point Review – summarize the Key Points of the Body. It is important to review the Key Points to increase listener retention.

Closing – communicate your POV, Specific Action Steps, and Benefit Summary along with your Memory Hook in the order that will have maximum listener impact.

Remember, above all else, the importance of making an emotional connection with your listeners. Speak genuinely and from the heart and you'll go a long way toward being most effective whenever you communicate.

EXAMPLE:

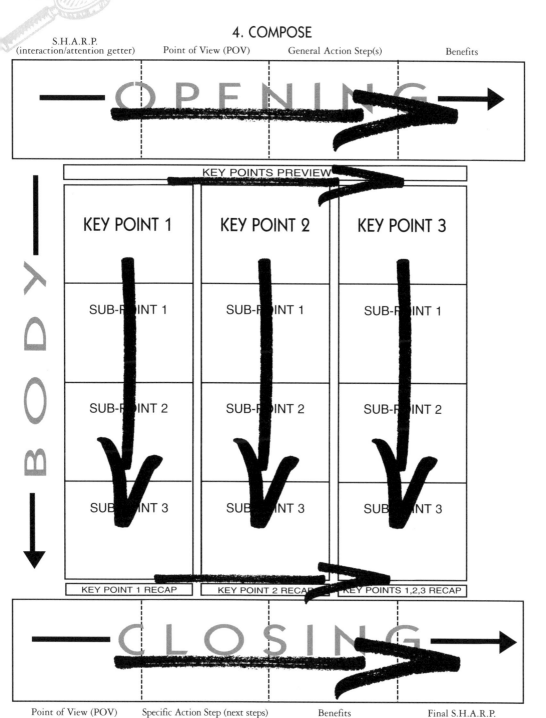

4. COMPOSE

S.H.A.R.P.
(interaction/attention getter)   Point of View (POV)   General Action Step(s)   Benefits

OPENING

KEY POINTS PREVIEW

BODY

KEY POINT 1   KEY POINT 2   KEY POINT 3

SUB-POINT 1   SUB-POINT 1   SUB-POINT 1

SUB-POINT 2   SUB-POINT 2   SUB-POINT 2

SUB-POINT 3   SUB-POINT 3   SUB-POINT 3

KEY POINT 1 RECAP   KEY POINT 2 RECAP   KEY POINTS 1,2,3 RECAP

CLOSING

Point of View (POV)   Specific Action Step (next steps)   Benefits   Final S.H.A.R.P.

APPLICATION ONE:
TIME FOR A QUICKIE!

When you have just five minutes to prepare, use the Quick Grid. For most of us, ample preparation time is a luxury we can rarely afford. When you have just minutes to prepare for a staff meeting or discussion with your manager, use the Quick Grid.

> **The Quick Grid streamlines the Create and Compose steps, thereby saving some time in preparation. To use the Quick Grid, lay the Cornerstones as usual. Then, instead of doing creative brainstorming for five minutes, simply write down the first three Key Points that come to mind. Put them in order of chronology or importance - with the most important last.**

Now brainstorm quickly on each Key Point in order to generate two or three Sub-points to support it.

You have now created the Body of your message in two to three minutes with Cornerstones to use in your Opening and Closing.

If everyone in the group or meeting has had little time to prepare, your ability to generate a Quick Grid will help you shine. Try it. We know you'll see the difference.

KEYS TO REMEMBER...
- Identify Subject and lay your Cornerstones
- Write down the first three Key Points that come to mind
- Quickly brainstorm each Key Point for one to three Sub-points
- Move Cornerstones to Opening and re-write them for Closing

APPLICATION TWO:
INCREASING YOUR PHONE POWER

The telephone is one of the places where people are least effective at communicating messages that motivate listeners.

When you call someone, do you take the moment necessary to establish the context (Cornerstones), collect your thoughts, and identify your Key Points? If you don't, you should. It will be the difference between communicating a net, action-oriented message, and rambling.

If you use The Decker Grid System® to create your message, you will be perceived as professional and credible. So what are you waiting for? Now that you have walked yourself through the process, use it to prepare for your next phone conversation.

The Decker Grid System® works whether you communicate with the person live on the phone or through a voicemail message. It works for both outgoing and incoming calls. If someone calls you, spend a few seconds at the beginning of the call identifying your Cornerstones on the subject being discussed.

APPLICATION THREE:
MAXIMIZING YOUR MEETING EFFECTIVENESS

Most of us spend far too much time in meetings. There are few things worse than sitting in an unproductive meeting, privately agonizing over the piles of work awaiting your return. Don't contribute to meeting mindlessness. Be a role model. Startle your associates by becoming a productive meeting contributor.

If you are the host of the meeting, use the Grid format to construct the actual agenda- from your POV for holding the meeting, to the actions you want your attendees to take, and the benefits to them. Your agenda items should be created from your Key Points.

If you are presenting a particular item on the agenda and you have some advance notice, prepare your complete message using the Grid format.

If you are called upon in a meeting without advance warning, ask for a moment to collect your thoughts and lay the Cornerstones of your message in your mind or on the paper in front of you.

Talkers have **ALWAYS** ruled. They will continue to rule. The smart thing is to join them. —Bruce Barton

KEYS TO REMEMBER...

• Begin with how you feel about the subject being introduced (POV).

• Ask yourself how the rest of the people in this meeting feel about the subject and your Point of View. What is their DNA? (Listener Cornerstone)

• What action do you want them to take to support your Point of View? (Action Steps)

• What benefits would there be for those at this meeting if they do as you suggest? (Benefits to listeners)

Simply by laying the Cornerstones, you will be able to articulate a concise, action-oriented message that will impress your fellow meeting attendees. And, you'll be more likely to get the results you want. That's how powerful this simple tool can be!

APPLICATION FOUR:
CREATING PRESENTATIONS THAT PRODUCE RESULTS

Your ability to inspire your listeners to take your desired action is the key to your success. Formal presentations are usually high-stakes situations in which you have much riding on the buy-in of your listeners. Don't waste this precious opportunity by communicating a less-than-powerful message.

You can't afford to be less than crystal clear. You must have punch and pizzazz and communicate a sincere Point of View. The last thing you want is for your listeners to be tuning out or thinking, "what is the point here?"

Formal presentations still involve one person communicating ideas persuasively to others. The key ingredients of The Decker Grid System® are as critical in this presentation format as in any other. In fact, in a high-stakes presentation, there is even more riding on your ability to impress, inform, and inspire your listeners to take action.

SOME HELPFUL HINTS IN MAXIMIZING YOUR PRESENTATION TIME

1   Use the 75% rule. When you practice your presentation from your completed Message Folder, take only 75% of your actual allotted time.

Why? Because invariably, in a real situation with questions and extrapolations, you will end up using more time than during your practice session. If your total rehearsal time is fifteen minutes, your actual presentation will run about twenty minutes.

2   Feel free to reference your notes. You should not feel the need to memorize every **Post-it® Note** nor should you hold your Message Folder in your hand. Simply place it nearby and, if necessary, pause, walk over to your notes, read the trigger words for the next section, move back to your speaking position, and begin speaking. Presenters are often uncomfortable with these silences; listeners, however, are not. It seems perfectly natural to watch someone pause to collect his or her thoughts. Try it and see!

3   Build in opportunities to involve your audience so that the communication is not all one-way. There are many ways to engage listeners, including asking questions, soliciting comments, and having listeners participate in exploring solutions with you.

4   Include Attention Getters and Memory Hooks, especially in your Opening and Closing. They can also be placed strategically in support of your Key Points. They may include one or more of the S.H.A.R.P. principles: **S**tories and Examples, **H**umor, **A**nalogies, **R**eferences and Quotes, **P**ictures/ Visual Aids.

APPLICATION FIVE:
HOSTING A SUCCESSFUL ALL-DAY MEETING OR SEMINAR

The Decker Grid System® is enormously effective in developing agendas for one or two-day meetings. In fact, at Decker Communications, all of our skill-building programs have Grids to guide our Consultants in their delivery.

To effectively develop and deliver a full-day communication event, follow these steps:

1 Develop your first Grid for the entire event. Carry out all of the steps including laying the Cornerstones, Creating, Clustering, and Composing.

2 Evaluate your Key Points: determine whether they should become actual modules or sections in your meeting or seminar. Then create a Grid based on that Key Point as the Grid subject.

When you lay the Cornerstones for this module, base it specifically on your POV, Listeners, Action Steps, and Benefits for the Key Point in question and, not for the entire day-long program.

3 Continue this process for each of your Key Points.

4 Once completed, you should have an overall Grid that maps out the entire day, and one Grid for each Key Point, or section of the day.

By using The Decker Grid System® to develop and deliver your all-day event, you will ensure that your participants receive a format that is listener-based and action-oriented. The information will be relevant to them and delivered in an interesting way that makes sense.

INTERACTING WITH YOUR VISUALS

One of the biggest mistakes communicators make is in failing to introduce their visual support. You should tell the audience what they are about to see.

It is also critical to PAUSE when displaying and then changing each visual. Listeners need at least a few seconds to orient themselves toward the new stimuli. If there are words on the visual, they need the time to read them before you begin speaking. And don't read the visuals to the audience.

We highly recommend building in blanks between your visuals to give you the time to re-focus the listeners on you, the communicator. Using PowerPoint®, you can simply hit the "B" key on your keyboard to make the screen blank.

Using Attention Getters and Memory Hooks effectively can make the difference between being a good communicator and an outstanding one. The Stories, Humor, Analogies, References/quotes, and Pictures/visual aids you use help ensure that your listeners have an interesting and informative experience when you communicate with them. By incorporating S.H.A.R.P.s into your message, you make it easier for your listeners to tune in and stay with you. You enhance the probability that they will remember the key elements of your message and will be more inspired to take your desired action.

USE IT OR LOSE IT

Taking skills from practice to application is the most challenging and rewarding part of the learning process. Make the commitment to yourself that the very next message you communicate will benefit from the enormous power of The Decker Grid System®. Whether it is a phone conversation, an agenda item at a meeting, or an hour-long presentation, your message will motivate your listeners to take action because it will contain all of the necessary ingredients for success. Those are:

FOUR CORNERSTONES TO SET THE CONTEXT
- A clear Point of View on your subject
- A message that is focused on your Listeners
- Clear, realistic, and measurable Action Steps for listeners
- Benefits to listeners for taking those actions

STRUCTURE TO HELP LISTENERS FOLLOW WHAT YOU ARE SAYING
- Three Key Points that are previewed, stated, and repeated
- Three Sub-points that give depth to each Key Point
- A powerful Opening and Closing to frame the Body of your message

ELEMENTS THAT ADD INTEREST AND HEART TO YOUR MESSAGE
- Attention Getters and Memory Hooks to boost listening and retention and connect you emotionally with your listeners. These are the S.H.A.R.P.s (Stories and Examples, Humor, Analogies, References and Quotes, and Pictures/Visual Aids).

We encourage you to accept the challenge of communicating memorable messages that motivate others to take action and get results. The Decker Grid System® will go a long way in getting you there as long as you use it and persevere.

For questions on The Decker Grid System® or any other Decker Communications' services, please call 1.800.547.0050 or visit our web site: http://www.decker.com.

Thank you for your interest in this information.

Bert Decker

Tools To Make You A More Effective Communicator.
Decker Communications is committed to helping you become more successful in your spoken communication. In addition to our consulting services and programs, we offer a variety of materials to assist you. To obtain more information, or to place an order for one of the following tools, please call us at 1.800.547.0050, send a fax to 415.391.7776, or visit our web site: http://www.decker.com.

SUCCESS GUIDE FOR CREATING MESSAGES THAT MOTIVATE
If you have found this Success Guide to be useful, why not order more for your associates and friends? It will take them through the steps to inspiring their listeners to take action and ensure that your time spent as a listener is more enjoyable, too!

Success Guide $24.95

SUCCESS KIT FOR CREATING MESSAGES THAT MOTIVATE
This Success Kit includes all the tools a person needs to succeed in every communication situation. It comes complete with a Success Guide, 3 additional Message Folders and **Post-it® Notes**.

Success Kit $29.95

MESSAGE FOLDERS
The Decker Grid System® helps you create messages that motivate. Our Message Folders help you work through the four-step process and serve as a reference when delivering your message. These handy re-usable folders come in packages of three.

Message Folder 3-Pack $3.95

BOOKS
You've Got To Be Believed To Be Heard
This book is full of examples and specific how-to exercises to improve your communication delivery. Spend a few evenings with this informative and entertaining book and you will learn how to win others' emotional trust - the true basis of communicating in business and in life.

Hardcover $21.95

Paperback $13.95

The Art Of Communicating

Is a highly interactive exploration of the behavioral skills that make a difference in how you are perceived as a communicator. Throughout its pages you will find checklists, worksheets, and exercises to increase your effectiveness.

Workbook $10.00

TAPES

High Impact Communication

This six-cassette album is designed to give you the executive edge in your communication skills. It explains the steps to becoming a confident speaker along with detailed exercises to improve the nine behavioral skills that impact your effectiveness. A must-have for every professional's audio library.

Audio Cassette Six-Pack $59.00

You've Got To Be Believed To Be Heard

This two-cassette program is the abridged version of the best-selling book. Learn to master the enormous power of the "First Brain" and use it to your advantage. Find out how to win others' emotional trust – the true basis of communicating successfully in business and in life.

Audio Cassette Two-Pack $15.95

VIDEO

How To Speak With Confidence

This video tutorial demonstrates the essential elements for speaking confidently to any size audience, in any setting. In 45 minutes you will watch and learn techniques to engage and involve your listeners and tools to help you create messages that speak to the heart.

Video $59.00

Volume discounts are available.

Call us at **1.800.547.0050** to find out the details!

Decker Communications helps businesses and individuals achieve their goals by improving the ways in which they communicate.

Our solutions range from corporate-wide communication of change to building the skills of individuals to be more effective face-to-face and on the phone.
- We work with executives to develop messages that focus on their listeners.
- We help businesses engage their people in the change process.
- We provide programs to build the skills people need to be effective communicators of important ideas.

Decker Communications is headquartered in San Francisco with offices nation-wide. The company is staffed with more than 100 dedicated professionals.

Since 1979, Decker Communications has improved the communications of over 100,000 professionals and hundreds of client companies.

For more information on how you can maximize the power of communication to transform your ideas into results, call 1.800.547.0050, or visit our web site:http://www.decker.com.

NOTES

NOTES